POSTMODERN ENCOUNTERS

Freud and False Memory Syndrome

Phil Mollon

Series editor: Richard Appignanesi

ICON BOOKS UK

TOTEM BOOKS

Published in the UK in 2000 by Icon Books Ltd., Grange Road, Duxford, Cambridge CB2 4QF email: info@iconbooks.co.uk www.iconbooks.co.uk

Published in the USA in 2000 by Totem Books Inquiries to: PO Box 223, Canal Street Station, New York, NY 10013

Distributed in the UK, Europe, Canada, South Africa and Asia by the Penguin Group: Penguin Books Ltd., 27 Wrights Lane, London W8 5TZ

In the United States, distributed to the trade by National Book Network Inc., 4720 Boston Way, Lanham, Maryland 20706

Published in Australia in 2000 by Allen & Unwin Pty. Ltd., PO Box 8500, 9 Atchison Street, St. Leonards, NSW 2065

Library of Congress catalog card number applied for

Series editor: Richard Appignanesi

ISBN 1 84046 133 0

Typesetting by Wayzgoose

Printed and bound in the UK by Cox & Wyman Ltd., Reading

False Memory Syndrome

In the early 1990s reports emerged of a new mental illness – false memory syndrome – in which people who had undergone psychotherapy or counselling came to 'remember' childhood abuse that had never actually happened. This was alleged to be an *iatrogenic* condition – that is, one produced by harmful medical or therapeutic practice.

The culprits were said to be psychotherapists who practice 'recovered memory therapy', based on a belief that many forms of adult distress and psychological difficulties may be caused by experiences of sexual abuse in childhood that had been forgotten or 'repressed'.

It was claimed that such therapists would encourage patients to search for repressed memories, perhaps with the aid of special techniques involving hypnosis.[1] Under the persuasive influence of the therapist, patients might come to believe in the reality of what were, in fact, imagined events, might cut themselves off from their family of origin and, even (in the USA), attempt to sue the alleged abuser, often the father. Protestations of innocence and bewilderment might be seen by the patient merely as evidence of the perpetrator's state of denial and inability to acknowledge his (or her) guilt. In these circumstances both the patient and the family could suffer unnecessarily as a result of misleading ideas promulgated in therapy.

When it became recognised that accusations of sexual abuse were becoming increasingly widespread, lobby groups were established to provide support for those accused, and also to promote awareness of the uncertainties of memory and disseminate information about 'false memory syndrome'.

Despite the existence of such organisations whose aim is to represent the interests of the relatives of those suffering from 'false memory syndrome', and the widespread coverage of this issue in both professional journals and the general media, it is surprisingly difficult to find a definition of the syndrome. Nor does it appear in any textbook of psychiatry, or any official listing of psychiatric or other medical conditions. However, John Kihlstrom, a cognitive psychologist and advisor to the False Memory Syndrome Foundation in the United States, has offered the following definition:

A condition in which a person's identity and interpersonal relationships are centered around a memory of traumatic experience which is objectively false but in which the person strongly believes. Note that the syndrome is not characterised by false memories as such . . . Rather, the syndrome may be diagnosed when the memory is so deeply engrained that it orientates the individual's entire personality and lifestyle, in turn disrupting all sorts of other adaptive behaviours . . . the person assiduously avoids confrontation with any evidence that might challenge the memory.[2]

This purported syndrome has not been validated, is not listed in official diagnostic texts and no clinical case studies outlining its features have been published in any medical or scientific journal. Nor are there any psychotherapists who would term themselves 'recovered memory therapists'. The depth and intensity of controversy over this issue would be difficult to exaggerate. A recent review text described the situation as follows:

From the very beginning, the debate has been characterised by a viciousness unparalleled in the annals of contemporary scientific disagreements. Because of the zealotry, science has taken a back seat. In its place have been wild and inaccurate articulations or 'hyperbole' and 'rhetorical devices' . . . that have served, not as science, but as emotional sound bites for a gullible media.[3]

Nevertheless, there are legitimate concerns about the reliability of memories of childhood and about misleading assumptions that may underlie the work of some psychotherapists.[4]

False beliefs and false accusations regarding experiences of sexual abuse can cause immense emotional damage and anguish. Our current knowledge of memory shows that it can be subject to a number of distortions. Remembering is recon-structive – like telling a story – rather than a process of accessing an accurate record of an event. It is, indeed, a plausible possibility that certain kinds of 'therapy' or styles of interview that involve sugges-tion, exhortations to remember, group pressure or abandonment of a critical and thoughtful perspec-tive by both patient and therapist could play on the deceptive plasticity of memory and lead to falla-cious narratives of a person's childhood.

However, these processes are complex, and there is considerable ongoing debate about what is involved in the forgetting and remembering of childhood trauma, and also about the nature and extent of harmful therapeutic practices.

Is Freud to Blame?

Those who promote the point of view of the false memory societies point to a number of factors to blame for the claimed epidemic of false memory syndrome. These include feminism, anti-men and anti-family attitudes, as well as a developing culture of victimhood, in which people are always looking for someone to blame for life's problems – and against whom there can be litigation. However, more specifically, they argue that a subculture of therapists has adopted unscientific beliefs and techniques – and that the ultimate figure to blame for this development is Freud. Thus, sociologists Ofshe and Watters remark:

All in all, Freud cut the very figure of a recovered memory therapist . . .

and

Freud proves to be the father of the recovered memory fad.[5]

Similarly, a professor of literature, Fred Crews, argues that Freud was the originator of recovered memory therapy and that:

[P]*sychoanalysis is the paradigmatic pseudoscience of our epoch.*[6]

So, was Freud the bad father who impregnated society with illegitimate fantasies, giving rise to the monster of false memory syndrome a hundred years later? Is it in Freud that we find the roots of the modern caricature of the 'recovered memory therapist', suggestively manipulating the mind and memory of the vulnerable patient, directing a search for recollections of trauma that never happened, believing that all manner of psychological problems have origins in childhood sexual abuse and holding hopelessly inaccurate views of memory? Or are such claims so at odds with the truth that they themselves invite psychoanalytic enquiry?

To answer these questions, we must consider Freud's observations and theorising regarding the causes of neurosis and also his views concerning memory.

Freud's Views on Psychopathology

Freud's first major publication, which marked the beginnings of psychoanalysis, was a book written jointly with Dr Josef Breuer called *Studies on Hysteria*.[7] In this, the authors described what was, at the time, the highly novel treatment – the 'talking cure'.

Freud and Breuer's discovery was that if the patient was encouraged to talk freely, it would often be possible to trace the origin of the symptom, which could then be understood in its interpersonal and psychodynamic context. This understanding would result in the resolution of the symptom.

The idea that talking could in itself cure hysterical disturbances of body function, such as paralysis, must have seemed astonishing when first presented.

Unfortunately, certain misperceptions of this book have been propagated then recycled in the current debates about recovered memory. For example, Daniel Schacter, an eminent research psychologist in the field of memory, stated the following:

Sigmund Freud and Josef Breuer's classic studies of hysteria described patients who could not explicitly remember childhood sexual abuse, but experienced disabling fears, nagging anxieties, intrusive thoughts, or disturbing images that reflected implicit memory for the trauma. However, these cases proved difficult to interpret because independent corroboration was often lacking.[8]

Such a claim is typical of the rhetoric of the false memory debate as part of the attempt to assimilate Freud into the category of 'recovered memory therapist'. However, it can only be based on a *fantasy* of what Freud and Breuer said rather than an actual reading of the text, for the five case histories do not concern problems resulting from childhood sexual abuse.

The Studies on Hysteria

The most famous of these cases, that of Anna O, does not actually relate at all to Freud's theory of psychoanalysis and his model of a mind in conflict. Instead, it illustrates Breuer's theory of 'hypnoid states' (spontaneously occurring states of self-hypnosis) as a basis for the dissociative symptoms of hysteria. The four other cases are Freud's. None concerns forgotten memories of childhood sexual abuse, although that of Katherina relates to a sexual assault at age fourteen.

Dammed up Libido

In the case of Emmy von N, Freud lists a number of traumas from her adult life which had given rise to her hysterical symptoms. For example, a dread of unexpected shocks was related to having seen her husband suffer a sudden heart attack; a fear of a stranger creeping into her room was linked to having entered a servant's room and seen a man hiding in the shadows; a fear of being buried alive related to her belief that her husband was not dead when his body was carried out.

Freud considered that the persistence of these anxieties resulted from her having lived for some years in a state of sexual abstinence. Thus, he viewed her as an illustration of his early theory (later largely abandoned) of *actual neuroses*, which were without psychological content but resulted from a psychosomatic condition of *dammed up libido*.

A Burnt Pudding

Lucy R was a governess who suffered from depression and an olfactory hallucination of a smell of *burnt pudding*. Freud encouraged her to remember the first occurrence of the smell. She reported that it had been two months previously when she had received a distressing letter from her mother and in her distraction had allowed a pudding to burn.

It emerged that Lucy R was experiencing a conflict at that time. She wanted to return to live with her mother, partly because she felt the other servants were gossiping about her, but also because she felt a sense of obligation to continue looking after the children, especially since she had promised their mother on her deathbed that she would do so.

As Freud enquired further, Lucy R revealed an additional context for her thoughts of leaving her employment. There had been an occasion in which her employer had confided in her, giving the impression of romantic interest and encouraging her desires and fantasies. However, this had been followed by an incident in which he had shouted at her and rudely reprimanded her, in such a way that her hopes of romance were crushed. It had been this humiliating blow to her self-esteem that led to her desire to leave.

Freud hypothesised that Lucy R's wish to leave her employment was incompatible with her desire to honour her promise to the children's mother and so this wish was repudiated, or 'repressed'. The repressed idea of leaving, which had probably been stimulated by the letter from her mother, left her conscious thought but an associated idea, the smell of burnt pudding, continually forced its way into her consciousness. Freud interpreted to Lucy R that she was in love with her employer. She acknowledged this, but added: 'I didn't know – or rather didn't want to know. I wanted to drive it out of my mind and not think about it again; and I believe latterly I have succeeded.' Freud comments in a footnote:

I have never managed to give a better description than this of the strange state of mind in which one knows and does not know a thing at the same time.[9]

The analysis, a remarkable example of brief psychotherapy, lasted nine weeks and had a happy outcome. Lucy R lost her symptoms of depression and olfactory hallucination, and accepted that her employer had no romantic interest in her.

Disagreeable Scenes

Katherina was an eighteen-year-old woman who approached Freud while he was holidaying in the mountains. She had been suffering from anxiety, breathlessness and a recurrent hallucination of an awful face. These symptoms had begun two years previously. When Freud suggested that she may have experienced something troubling two years ago, she replied: 'Heavens yes – that was when I caught my uncle with that girl Franziska, my cousin.'

It emerged that on seeing her uncle and cousin in a sexual embrace she had become breathless and also suffered vomiting. As Freud encouraged her to keep talking, she reported that her uncle had also made sexual advances to her when she was fourteen – but owing to naiveté she had not recognised these as sexual assaults at the time. Freud concluded that when Katherina had seen her uncle and Franziska together sexually, she had thought: 'Now he's doing with her what he wanted to do with me that night and those other times.'

Katherina agreed with this reconstruction. Thus the trauma was retrospective, evoked by the later realisation of the *meaning* of her uncle's behaviour. It also emerged that Katherina had reported the sight of her uncle and Franziska to her aunt and this had led to '*disagreeable scenes*' between her uncle and aunt. Her uncle had raged at Katherina and it turned out that his was the 'awful face' that Katherina had hallucinated. In a footnote dated 1924, Freud ventures to 'lift the veil of discretion' and reveal that Katherina's uncle was in fact her father!

Pains in the Legs

Elizabeth von R suffered from pains in her legs and difficulties in walking – symptoms that were considered hysterical. As Freud followed her trains of thought, she recalled a situation of emotional conflict during a time when she had been nursing her sick father. She had been out at a party and was escorted home by a young man to whom she was very attracted. However, when she returned to her father she found him in a much worse state and then reproached herself for having neglected him.

With further analytic exploration, another similar conflict emerged, from a few years later. Apparently, she had been attracted to her brother-in-law and subsequently her sister died during pregnancy. Freud interpreted that Elizabeth von R must have thought that her brother-in-law would now be free to marry her, then have felt so guilty about this thought that she had immediately repudiated or repressed the idea. He argued that in each of these situations of psychical conflict, Elizabeth von R had experienced the erotic thought and desire as incompatible with her conscious morality, and therefore the idea had been repressed and the associated affect turned into sensations of pain.

The patient was cured by the analysis. She did not marry the brother-in-law, but someone else. Freud reports that he subsequently attended a ball where she was also a guest and he witnessed her 'whirl past me in a lively dance', her leg problems clearly resolved.

Commentary

Contrary to Schacter's assertion, the cases in the *Studies* do not concern repression of memory, nor recovered memory, and are not related to childhood sexual abuse. Instead, the four cases treated by Freud are all presented as examples of emotional conflict and trauma, resulting in undischarged and dammed up affect or libido. The hysterical symptoms are seen as displaced expressions of the blocked affect or libido. Thus, Emmy von N was seen as suffering from traumatic stress combined with undischarged libido resulting from her sexual abstinence. Lucy R, suffering from the pain of unrequited love, was torn between her wish to return home to her mother and her loyalty to the children in her care and to their mother. Katherina had experienced the shock of seeing her father in bed with her cousin, realising that this must have been what he had wanted to do with her when he had tried to get into her bed a couple of years previously. Elizabeth von R felt guilty because she had wanted to marry her brother-in-law after her sister had died and so had repressed this wish.

The case study of Emmy von N seems the least satisfactory. It is not apparent what emotional conflict she was struggling with and thus the *psychodynamic* explanation is lacking. Freud implies that he sees her as an example of his concept of an actual neurosis, the syndrome of those who fall ill directly through a lack of sexual satisfaction. By contrast, the three others were suffering from painful emotional conflicts and dilemmas involving desire, guilt and shame – states of anguish which the reader could readily understand. These women probably had very limited opportunity to share or voice their conflicts, to themselves or others. Denied access to speech, their pain found expression in the body, until liberated into language through a healing conversation with Freud.

None of these cases, as described by Freud, involved repression of memory. The objects of repression were thoughts, feelings and desires.

Freud's Sexual Abuse Theory of Psychopathology

Freud did briefly hold a theory of a sexual abuse aetiology (or causation) for hysteria. It is contained in two papers, both dated 1896. The first is *Further Remarks on the Neuropsychoses of Defence*. He begins by stating that he has grouped together a number of psychopathic states under the general term 'the neuro-psychoses of defence', explaining that they all have in common the fact that:

[T]*heir symptoms arose through the psychical mechanism of (unconscious)* defence – *that is, in an attempt to repress an incompatible idea which had come into distressing opposition to the patient's ego.*[10]

Freud builds upon his earlier view, stated in the *Studies*, that the symptoms of hysteria can be traced back to psychical traumas, but he then goes further in arguing that:

[T]*hese sexual traumas must have occurred in early childhood (before puberty) and their content must consist of an actual irritation of the genitals (of processes resembling copulation).*[11]

Interestingly, he argues that the reason hysteria is more common in women is because female children are more likely to be victims of sexual assault – although he does mention two cases of male hysteria.

The Two Trauma Theory

Freud did not consider that the sexual molesting of children was in itself necessarily harmful at the time. He comments:

Sexual assaults on small children happen too often for them to have any aetiological importance.[12]

Instead, he theorised that the pathogenic effect of childhood sexual abuse occurred when a later trauma (after puberty) threatened to re-evoke the memory of the earlier assault. He argued that while the genesis of hysteria requires direct stimulation of the child's own genitals, the later trauma that re-evokes the memory of the earlier assault can be of various kinds relating to sexuality

. . . from actual sexual violation to mere sexual overtures or the witnessing of sexual acts in other people, or receiving information about sexual processes.[13]

The memory itself is repressed and the associated affect is converted into the hysterical symptom. Furthermore, he hypothesised at this point that memory of a later sexual assault (occurring after puberty) will only happen if the experience activates a memory of a related trauma in childhood.

A Fear of Shops

This deferred action of trauma, whereby the later experience re-evokes the earlier one, resulting in symptoms, is also discussed in Freud's *Project for a Scientific Psychology* (1895) – his early attempt to integrate psychology and neurology. He gives a clinical example of a patient, Emma, who was unable to go into shops alone. She produced a memory from age twelve, when she went into a shop and saw two male assistants laughing at her clothes, one of whom she found attractive. She had run out of the shop in anxiety. Freud reported that 'further investigation' revealed a second memory: at age eight she had been sexually molested by the owner of a sweet shop. An associative link between these two scenes was the laughing of the shop assistants, which had reminded Emma of the grin of the shop keeper as he had grabbed at her genitals. Another link was that she had gone into each shop alone. Freud explains what happened when the first memory (from age eight) was re-evoked:

The memory aroused what it was certainly not able to at the time, a sexual release, which was transformed into anxiety. With this anxiety, she was afraid that the shop-assistants might repeat the assault, and she ran away.[14]

Freud adds that the detail in the second memory (from age twelve), concerning Emma's finding one of the shop assistants attractive, indicated the emergence of the sexual release into her consciousness, albeit disconnected from its link to the first memory.

Deferred Action

In one sense the notion of 'deferred action' relates to an everyday clinical observation, familiar to those who work with patients abused in childhood. Anxiety and other emotions associated with sexual trauma are evoked when an event in adulthood provides a link to the childhood trauma. A common example is when a person who was sexually abused as a child later has a child of his or her own, or when their child reaches an age at which that person had originally been abused. However, today we would tend to understand this effect in two ways, neither of which seems to have been Freud's meaning.

First, the adult event directly evokes the childhood experience which was, in its own right, traumatic (for example, frightening, over-stimulating, confusing).

Second, the adult brings his or her greater sexual awareness to bear on the childhood experience and endows it with a traumatic meaning that it might not have had at the time.

What Freud meant, however, was that the childhood memory, now evoked after puberty, gives rise to sexual arousal which the original event had not done. This sexual energy, libido, is not experienced directly as sexuality but is transformed physiologically into anxiety. At this point in his theorising, Freud thought that anxiety came about through the damming up of libido and its resulting transformation when denied normal expression. Moreover, he had not yet begun to theorise about childhood sexuality and the child's own desires.

Freud also applies his theory of defence to obsessional neurosis and paranoid schizophrenia.[15] In both these cases, the symptoms represent the *return of the repressed* in displaced and disguised form. What is repressed might be an affect, an idea or a memory. In the case of an obsessive-compulsive neurosis, the patient also engages in compulsive actions which have a protective function, aiding in the ego's struggle against the repressed.

A Bedtime Ritual

Freud gives an example of obsessive-compulsive protective measures in the case of an eleven-year-old boy whose bedtime rituals included the following. He would not go to sleep until he had told his mother in minute detail about the events of the day; he had to ensure there were no pieces of paper or other rubbish on the carpet; his bed had to be placed right against the wall; three chairs had to be placed in front of it; the pillows had to lie in a particular way; he had to kick his legs out a certain number of times and then lie on his side.

Freud explained that some years previously a servant girl had sexually abused the boy in his bed. Later, a more recent event re-evoked the memory which

. . . *manifested in his consciousness in a compulsion to perform the ceremonial.*[16]

Thus, the boy did not consciously remember the original sexual abuse but *instead* experienced the compulsion to perform the ritual, which functioned as a protection against any possibility of a repeat of the sexual trauma. The ritual contained the following meaning: the chairs were arranged so that no one could get to the bed; the pillows were arranged differently from how they were when he was abused; the kicking was to push away the girl lying on top of him; sleeping on his side was to contrast with the position he was lying in when he was abused; his detailed confession of the day's events was in rebellion against his seductress' prohibiting the telling of what had taken place; his preoccupation with keeping his bedroom floor clean was because a failure to do so was a source of reproach from his mother – reflecting his fear of reproach about the sexual activity.

A Case of Paranoia

Freud also applied his theory of repression and return of the repressed to the case of a woman suffering from severe paranoid schizophrenia. Frau P was thirty-two years of age, and married with a child of two. She fell ill with psychosis six months after the birth of her child, becoming withdrawn and distrustful and complaining that people were against her. As her illness worsened, she began to believe she was being watched and that people were reading her thoughts. One day she developed the idea that she was being watched while undressing. Later she began to experience hallucinations of naked women. Moreover, when she was in the presence of another woman she would imagine that the woman was seeing a picture of *her* naked. She also heard voices commenting on her actions.

Freud applied his method of exploring the origins of these symptoms. He found that the hallucinations of naked women had begun after she had been sent for treatment at a hydropathic establishment where she would, in fact, have seen naked women in the baths. Frau P reported great shame at the thought of nakedness. Freud reasoned that the experience of shame must be an obsessional reaction to an earlier experience which had *not* originally been associated with shame. Frau P recalled a number of scenes going back to her eighth year in which she had felt shame about appearing naked in front of her family or the doctor. However, this culminated in a memory from age six when she was undressing in front of her brother without a sense of shame. It then transpired that Frau P and her brother had often been in the habit of exhibiting themselves naked to each other before going to bed. Thus, Freud reasoned, Frau P's sudden idea that she was being watched while undressing had been

. . . an unaltered piece of the old memory which involved self-reproach, and she was now making up for the shame which she had omitted to feel as a child.[17]

Gradually, more details emerged of a quite extensive sexual relationship with her brother, lasting at least from her sixth to her tenth year. Frau P revealed that when she became married she had developed a great aversion to sex and was very worried that the noises of her sexual activity with her husband might be heard by the neighbours through the party-wall. Freud interpreted that the beginning of her marriage had unconsciously awakened her childhood affair in which she and her brother had played at husband and wife, and that this had resulted in self-reproaches which were repressed. The hallucinatory voices were a disguised version of these repressed self-reproaches about her sexual experiences. While seemingly innocuous in content, they subtly expressed reproach. In this way they were a compromise between the forces of repression and those of the returning repressed.

Freud gives a detailed account of Frau P's reactions of depression and the onset of her paranoia. The depression began after a quarrel between her husband and her brother, as a result of which her brother stopped visiting. Following this, there had been an occasion when 'everything became clear' to her that she was despised by everyone. This took place during a conversation with her sister-in-law who happened to use the words: 'If anything of that sort happens to me, I treat it in light vein.'

Afterwards, Frau P took the words as some kind of reproach against her, although she could not be clear in what way. She concluded that it must have been the tone of voice in which her sister-in-law had spoken the words. Freud asked her to recall what was said just before this remark and Frau P remembered that her sister-in-law had commented that in her parents' home there had been all kinds of problems with brothers – and had then said: 'In every family all sorts of things happen that one would like to draw a veil over. But if anything of the kind happens to *me*, I take it lightly.'

Freud explains that Frau P had repressed this earlier statement referring to brothers because it might have re-awakened a memory of her sexual relationship with her brother – and had instead become preoccupied with the second statement. Her sense of being reproached, which really belonged to the sexual relationship with her brother, became attached to the remark about taking things lightly, an example of displacement. Since the content of the remark does not contain any obvious reproach, Frau P concluded that it was the tone of voice that was reproachful. Freud indicated that this was an example of how the misinterpretations of the paranoid person can be based on repression.

Positively Revolting

Freud concludes that hysteria, obsessional neurosis and paranoia all have similar origins.

In each of them, repression has been shown to be the nucleus of the psychical mechanism, and in each what has been repressed is a sexual experience in childhood.[18]

He states that all his thirteen cases were severe and that the childhood traumas involved 'grave sexual injuries', some of which were 'positively revolting'. The perpetrators of the abuse were

. . . nursemaids, governesses and domestic servants, to whose care children are only too thoughtlessly entrusted; teachers, moreover, figure with regrettable frequency.[19]

However, in seven of these cases, 'blameless children were the assailants', mainly brothers who had for years played out sexual activities with sisters a little younger. In some cases, the boy had earlier been sexually abused by a female and then some years later he would enact sexual aggression towards his sister along the same lines that he had been abused.

Freud described how the sexual abuse could reverberate and repeat within families. In one instance, a brother, a sister and a male cousin were all neurotically ill. It turned out, from the analysis of the brother, that he suffered self-reproaches for having caused his sister's illness through abusing her; he himself had been abused by the cousin who, in turn, had been abused by the nursemaid.

The Aetiology of Hysteria

. . . hysterical symptoms are derivatives of memories which are operating unconsciously.[20]

A few weeks after the paper on the neuropsychoses of defence was written, Freud produced another paper based on a lecture to an audience of psychiatrists and neurologists. *The Aetiology of Hysteria* reaffirms and builds on his previous observations and conclusions, but in a manner typical of Freud as he addresses an audience, he anticipates many of the likely objections and criticisms.

Chains of Memory

Freud begins with the discovery that he attributes to his earlier colleague Josef Breuer:

The symptoms of hysteria . . . are determined by certain experiences of the patient's which have operated in a traumatic fashion and which are being reproduced in his psychical life in the form of mnemonic symbols.[21]

He then argues that tracing a hysterical symptom back to a traumatic scene is relevant only if this scene has two characteristics: it must be *suitable* to act as a determinant, in that its content bears some connection to the content of the symptom; and it must possess sufficient *traumatic force*.

Moreover, he explains that usually the initial traumatic scene that is uncovered does *not* appear to possess both these characteristics. This means that the analytic work has to proceed further back, following the train of associations, to find a second traumatic scene hidden behind the first. In fact, he concludes, a hysterical symptom is never produced by one actual experience but instead is a result of the reactivation of a memory of a traumatic earlier experience.

Freud describes complex associative chains of memories that link various symptoms; he likens these to the genealogical tree of a family whose members have inter-married. However, he states his unequivocal conclusion:

Whatever case and whatever symptom we take as our point of departure, in the end we infallibly come to the field of sexual experience.[22]

Freud argues that while the precipitating later scenes may be quite varied in their reference to sexuality, the earlier traumatic scenes always involve sexual abuse of the child's body. He claims as follows:

If we have the perseverance to press on with the analysis into early childhood, as far back as a human memory is capable of reaching, we invariably bring the patient to reproduce experiences which, on account both of their peculiar features and of their relations to the symptoms of his later illness, must be regarded as the aetiology of his neurosis for which we have been looking. These infantile experiences are once more sexual in content, but they are of a far more uniform kind than the scenes at puberty that had been discovered earlier.[23]

Repellent Scenes

Anticipating the sense of disgust and revulsion of his audience, Freud expresses his own. He states:

[T]he idea of these infantile sexual scenes is very repellent to the feelings of a sexually normal individual; they include all the abuses known to debauched and impotent persons, among whom the buccal cavity and the rectum are misused for sexual purposes.[24]

Freud goes on to explain that the perverse nature of the sexual acts is understandable once it is considered that a person who is prepared to satisfy his (or her) sexual desires with children is unlikely to be too fussy about the means of sexual satisfaction. He regards these activities as the acts of impotent persons who are unable to engage in normal sexual activity with an adult of the opposite sex. In this respect he regards them as similar to the children who are abused, and who also are impotent sexually. It is perhaps of interest to note that in the social and cultural context of Freud's day, oral sex (involving the 'buccal cavity') appears to have been considered 'debauched'.

Freud reveals an understanding of the long-term effects of sexual abuse, which is consistent with today's awareness. For example, he wrote the following insightful comment on the power imbalance between child and abuser and the perversion of the role of authority:

All the singular conditions under which the ill-matched pair conduct their love-relations – on the one hand the adult, who cannot escape his share in the mutual dependence necessarily entailed by a sexual relationship, and who is yet armed with complete authority and the right to punish, and can exchange the one role for the other to the uninhibited satisfaction of his moods, and on the other hand the child, who in his helplessness is at the mercy of this arbitrary will, who is prematurely aroused to every kind of sensibility and exposed to every sort of disappointment, and whose performance of the sexual activities assigned to him is often interrupted by his imperfect control of his natural needs – all these grotesque and yet tragic incongruities reveal them-

selves as stamped upon the later development of his neurosis, in countless permanent effects which deserve to be traced in the greatest detail.[25]

Reality of the Sexual Scenes?

Freud describes the evidence for his conclusions. He reports that he had now worked with eighteen patients who suffer from 'neuroses of defence' and who show this aetiology. Each of these has involved 'in most cases up to a hundred or more hours of work'.[26] Thus, he argues, his conclusions cannot be regarded as the 'fruit of idle speculation'.[27]

He also addresses the evidence for the 'reality of infantile sexual scenes'. He is, in fact, highly alert to the question of whether these sexual scenes are real or imaginary, anticipating the scepticism of his audience, and he lists a number of factors supporting his conclusion that they are veridical.

First, he notes a certain uniformity of detail in the accounts from various patients, even though they have not been in discussion with each other and there were no group pressures or any culture focusing on recovered memories of abuse.

Second, the patients sometimes describe as harmless, events whose significance they do not appreciate, or details, mentioned in passing

. . . which only someone of experience in life can understand and appreciate as subtle traits of reality.[28]

Furthermore, the impression of veridicality is supported by the relationship of the sexual scenes to the overall case history. Freud draws an analogy with a jigsaw puzzle – there is only one piece that fits exactly. However, Freud argues that there would be one other proof – 'a really unassailable one' – the corroboration of the material of the person being analysed by the evidence of *someone else*. This is actually the standard of proof requested by those who support today's false memory societies.

One example of this corroboration is where two children have had a childhood sexual relationship with each and one subsequently confirms the memories of the other. Freud states that he found this kind of corroboration in two of his eighteen cases.

In one case a brother confirmed his childhood sexual activity with his sister. The second case involved two women who both had childhood sexual relations with the same man and also with each other in a threesome. Both women suffered the same symptom, which Freud saw as derived from the childhood events.

Freud anticipates two contrasting objections to his conclusion that sexual experiences in childhood, involving direct stimulation of the genitals and 'coitus-like acts', are the fundamental traumas that are re-evoked by later traumas at or after puberty, and which then give rise to hysterical symptoms.

One argument would be that sexual abuse of children is such a rare event that it cannot plausibly be regarded as the determinant of such a common syndrome as hysteria.

The other opposite argument would be to claim that such experiences are so common that for this reason they cannot be of aetiological significance, especially since it is not difficult to find people who have suffered sexual abuse in childhood and have not fallen ill with hysteria.

Regarding the first objection, Freud argues that children are far more often exposed to sexual assaults than is generally recognised, and he cites publications by paediatricians that draw attention to the frequency of sexual practices by nurses and nursery maids, carried out on even young babies.

He divides his eighteen cases into three groups, according to the perpetrators of the childhood sexual assaults. In the first group are the assaults by adults who were strangers; in the second are those assaults by an adult in a position of care for the child, such as a nursery maid, or governess, or tutor 'or, unhappily all too often, a close relative', who initiated the child into a sexual relationship that lasted for years; in the third are the sexual relationships between children, mostly a brother and sister, and which are often prolonged beyond puberty.

Freud added that in most of his cases two or more of these aetiologies operated together. He continues:

In a few instances the accumulation of sexual experiences coming from different quarters was truly amazing.[29]

However, he comments that this surprising observation may be more understandable when it is appreciated that his patients were all suffering from 'severe neurotic illness which threatened to make life impossible'.[30]

Freud provides the further interesting observation that where there had been a relationship between two children, he sometimes found that the boy who initiated the sexual activity had previously been seduced by an adult female and that he had subsequently tried to repeat with the little girl exactly the same activities that the adult had performed on him.

Freud then turns to the second possible objection to his hypothesis of the role of sexual trauma in childhood, namely that sexual abuse of children is extremely common and that not all who have such experiences subsequently suffer hysteria. He argues that it does not matter to his hypothesis if many people experience sexual abuse in childhood without becoming hysterics, providing that all those who *do* become hysterics have experienced such abuse. He draws an analogy with smallpox: not everyone who is in contact with a smallpox victim develops the disease, but infection by a patient is the only known cause of the disease. He makes the further point that the hypothesis of the aetiological significance of childhood sexual trauma is not based solely upon its occurrence in the childhoods of hysterics, but upon there being 'associative and logical ties' between the scenes of abuse and the hysterical symptoms.

Could the Scenes be False Memories?

Freud is highly alert to the alternative hypothesis that the apparent memories of childhood sexual abuse are false memories evoked by an authoritative doctor and a compliant patient. He asks rhetorically:

Is it not very possible either that the physician forces such scenes upon his docile patients, alleging that they are memories, or else that the patients tell the physician things which they have deliberately invented or have imagined and that he accepts those things as true?[31]

He presents a number of arguments against this. First, he states that before they come for analysis, the patients are unaware consciously of the childhood memories of abuse, which are recalled only through 'the strongest compulsion of the treatment'.[32] While recalling them they experience distress and 'violent sensations' and shame. Moreover, even after reliving the scenes in a very convincing manner, they still attempt to deny their reality. Freud asks:

Why should patients assure me so emphatically of their unbelief, if what they want to discredit is something which – from whatever motive – they themselves have invented?[33]

He acknowledges that it is less easy to refute the suspicion that he has influenced the patients to imagine these scenes and present them as memories through the influence of suggestion. Nevertheless, Freud regards this as untenable. He states:

I have never yet succeeded in forcing on a patient a scene I was expecting to find, in such a way that he seemed to be living through it with all the appropriate feelings.[34]

What Freud does not specify in this paper is the means by which the patient is induced to recall the unconscious memories. He indicates that they are not revealed freely and that they are produced against the resistance of the patient. However, in a section written by Freud alone in the jointly authored book with Breuer, he describes his method. He states that he began with exploration through hypnosis, just as other hysteria physicians of the time had done, but found that this was not successful with all patients.

Accordingly, he developed a method of asking patients to concentrate and remember the first occurrence of the symptom, then following the chain of associations back in time. This was supplemented by the device of telling patients that when he pressed upon their foreheads, they would remember something. In this and various related ways, Freud would endeavour to help patients put aside their conscious wills and allow unexpected ideas, images and memories to come to mind. He noted that it is rare for the crucial pathogenic memories to emerge clearly and easily. Instead what is found are intermediate links in a chain of associations – and these links are often broken and fragmented.

Looking back from a later period of an analysis to an earlier one, we are often astonished to realise in what a mutilated manner all the ideas and scenes emerged which we extracted from the patient by the procedure of pressing.[35]

This, then, was the method that Freud presumably was using at the time he wrote *The Aetiology of Hysteria*. Undoubtedly, such a method would not be advisable in the light of today's knowledge of the propensity for hypnotism and related methods to generate confabulation rather than authentic memories. Nevertheless, Freud describes his method and rationale with considerable clarity and elaborate thought. His own emphasis was upon his recognition of the patient's *resistance* to remembering, a manifestation of the *defence* nature of the hysteria – and his assumption that the physician's task was to overcome this resistance.

Congruence with Current Perspectives

The Aetiology of Hysteria is a remarkable paper, brilliant yet fundamentally flawed. At the time of writing, Freud had not yet come to appreciate the shifting, misleading and treacherous nature of memory and its tendency to mate with phantasy and give birth to confabulation. Nevertheless – in his understanding of the prevalence of childhood sexual abuse, its profound pathological effects, the phenomenon of identification with the aggressor (whereby the abused becomes an abuser), as well as in his grasp of how an adult trauma may obtain its impact by re-evoking an earlier trauma – in so many ways Freud's insights are remarkably close to some of our perspectives a hundred years later. This is so, even though his ideas would have seemed incongruent with the consensus for most of the 20th century, since the current recognition of the prevalence and impact of child sexual abuse, and the understanding of trauma effects, are quite recent.

Freud's Abandonment of the 'Seduction Theory'

Although Freud did abandon the essential theory of a sexual abuse aetiology of hysteria, he did not entirely dismiss his recognition of the prevalence and impact of sexual trauma in childhood. For example, in a footnote to *The Aetiology of Hysteria*, added later in 1924 and attached to his description of the process of recollection of the scenes of abuse against the resistance of the patient, he wrote:

All this is true; but it must be remembered that at the time I wrote it I had not yet freed myself from my overvaluation of reality and my low valuation of phantasy.[36]

His later position is elaborated further in a footnote, also dated 1924, added to his paper *Further Remarks on the Neuropsychoses of Defence*:

This section is dominated by an error which I have since repeatedly acknowledged and corrected. At that time I was not yet able to distinguish between my patients' phantasies about their childhood years and their real recollections. As a result, I attributed to the aetiological factor of seduction a significance and universality which it does not possess. When this error had been overcome it became possible to obtain an insight into the spontaneous manifestations of the sexuality of children which I described

in my Three Essays on the Theory of Sexuality
*(1905). Nevertheless, we need not dismiss every-
thing written in the text above. Seduction retains a
certain aetiological importance, and even today I
think some of these psychological comments are to
the point.*[37]

This comment seems very fair, and one with which
the majority of psychoanalytically informed practi-
tioners would find themselves in agreement.
Seduction or sexual abuse of children does play a
part in the development of some psychological
problems, but it does not have an essential and universal aetiological significance. Moreover, phantasies about childhood can be misperceived as true
recollections.

In his paper, *On the History of the Psycho-
Analytical Movement*, published in 1914, Freud
refers again to his 'mistaken idea', which he notes
'might have been almost fatal to the young science'.
He explains that analysis had correctly led back
from present-day symptoms to something in the
past, but he had mistakenly been inclined to accept
as true the scenes of sexual seduction that had eventually emerged, especially since he had not at that
time developed his theories of childhood sexuality.

He further notes that when he felt forced to abandon this aetiological hypothesis, 'under the weight of its own improbability and contradiction in definitely ascertainable circumstances', his reaction was one of 'helpless bewilderment' and he would 'gladly have given up the whole work' since 'the firm ground of reality was gone'.[38]

However, following his sense of despair, he recognised that if his expectations had turned out to be false, then he must revise them, and this led to a new insight.

If hysterical subjects trace back their symptoms to traumas that are fictitious, then the new fact which emerges is precisely that they create such scenes in phantasy, and this psychical reality requires to be taken into account alongside practical reality.[39]

Thus, Freud was led to his theory of childhood sexuality, the Oedipus complex and the pervasive role of phantasy, psychical reality and self-deception in mental life.

Some recent commentators have argued that Freud dishonestly distorted the true situation regarding his change of mind.[40] They argue that Freud first coerced his patients into producing false scenes of childhood sexual abuse, which were really his own inventions, and then, realising his error, he subsequently claimed that his patients had spontaneously told him of their sexual scenes, and in this way had given him the idea of childhood sexuality and the Oedipus complex.

They further point out that originally Freud claimed the sexual abusers were nursemaids, governesses and so on, but later claimed that most of his patients had said they were abused by their fathers – a claim, it is alleged, that would have been convenient for his account of how he discovered the Oedipus complex whereby the child desires the father or mother in phantasy.

These points have little substance. They are all covered by Freud's actual texts and his later footnotes. He freely admits that in early papers he played down the role of seduction by fathers because the idea would seem too disturbing to his readers (as well as perhaps to himself). His change of mind about how crucial sexual abuse was can be seen as part of a wider and consistent pattern whereby Freud continually revised his views in the light of his further clinical experience and thought.

Despite his abandonment of the 'seduction theory' of hysteria, Freud continued at times to indicate an awareness of the pathogenic role of childhood sexual abuse in some cases. For example, in his *Moses and Monotheism*, he discusses the impact of psychological traumas in general and comments in passing,

A girl who was made the object of a sexual seduction in early childhood may direct her later sexual life so as constantly to provoke similar attacks.[41]

In another late paper, published in 1940 (*Splitting of the Ego*), Freud gives a clinical example of how a little boy can come to believe in the 'reality' of a threat of castration. He explains that the little boy, aged three, 'had become acquainted with the female genitals through being seduced by an older girl' and that afterwards he had 'carried on the sexual stimulation set going in this way by zealously practising manual masturbation', which led to his 'energetic nurse' threatening him with castration.[42]

Freud's reason for presenting this example is to illustrate how the boy's previous sight of the female genitals and the absence of a penis, combined with the threat of castration, could convince the child that the threat was real. However, what is interesting from the present point of view is that the idea of childhood sexual abuse is almost casually woven into this illustration.

Truth and Falsehood

Freud continued to see recovered memories as likely to comprise truth and falsehood, and he points to this inherent tension, which defies resolution, in the following starkly articulated passage.

If the infantile experiences brought to light by analysis were invariably real, we should feel that we were standing on firm ground; if they were regularly falsified and revealed as inventions, as phantasies of the patient, we should be obliged to abandon this shaky ground and look for salvation elsewhere. But neither of these things is the case: the position can be shown to be that the childhood experiences constructed or remembered in analysis are sometimes indisputably false and sometimes equally certainly correct, and in most cases compounded of truth and falsehood.[43]

Sexual Abuse is 'Common Enough'

Freud also indicates the importance of childhood sexual abuse in one of his last papers summarising his views: *An Outline of Psycho-Analysis*, published in 1940. He comments on the effects of certain experiences which, while not universal, are 'common enough'. These are listed as:

[T]*he sexual abuse of children by adults, their seduction by other children (brothers or sisters) slightly their seniors, and, what we should not expect, their being deeply stirred by seeing or hearing at first hand sexual behaviour between adults (their parents) mostly at a time at which one would not have thought they could either be interested in or understand any such impressions, or be capable of remembering them later.*[44]

Freud states that such experiences

. . . arouse a child's susceptibility and force his own sexual urges into certain channels from which they cannot afterwards depart.[45]

He notes furthermore that such early impressions, of traumatic sexual over-stimulation, are subject to repression when they threaten to return as memories and therefore give rise to 'the neurotic compulsion which will subsequently make it impossible for the ego to control the sexual function', the result being either sexual inhibition or sexual perversion.

These comments on sexual trauma in childhood are presented briefly and in passing, as Freud moves on to his greater concern with the Oedipus complex. Nevertheless, the fact that they are there in this late paper indicates that, notwithstanding the criticisms of Masson (1984), Freud retained an unblinkered view of the reality of sexual abuse in some cases and of its terrible developmental consequences.

Freud's View of Memory

It is sometimes asserted that Freud held that events of a person's life were all recorded accurately somewhere in the mind, like a continual video-recording, ready to be accessed if only the memories could be released from repression. Is there any evidence that he held this view?

Memory in Dreams

In what is possibly Freud's most famous book, *The Interpretation of Dreams* (published in 1900 but apparently written largely by 1896), he discusses the way that dreams draw upon memory. He comments:

No one who occupies himself with dreams can, I believe, fail to discover that it is a very common event for a dream to give evidence of knowledge and memories which the waking subject is unaware of possessing.[46]

He gives many examples of this. In one of Freud's own dreams, he sees a man whom he knows (in the dream) is a doctor in his native town; the face is indistinct but confused with that of a teacher at his secondary school. Enquiries with his mother revealed that there had been such a doctor during Freud's early childhood and that he had had one eye; the schoolmaster too had one eye and this was the dream link between the two. Freud had not actually seen the doctor for thirty-eight years and had no conscious memory of him.

However, Freud emphasises that although dreams draw upon diverse material from memory, giving the impression that all experience which is initially registered may in principle be available for recall, dreams usually present only fragments of reproductions and mix details from one experience with those from another in such a way that disregards external reality.

Here is a crucial point revealed by Freud's observations of dreams. All kinds of impressions from experiences throughout life may be stored in some way within the brain and are available for use by dreams, but this does not mean that it is possible to recover those memories in a conscious, coherent and accurate form. On the whole, dreams do not reproduce but scramble. For Freud, dreams were about disguised expressions of wish fulfilment, distortion derived from internal conflict, 'a kind of inner dishonesty'.[47]

If dreams are a form of repudiation of reality, scavenging elements promiscuously from diverse experiences and impressions, they can hardly be viewed as a route to the discovery of historical reality.

The startling implications of this are taken a step further when Freud demonstrates how memories, especially of events of long ago, may be constructed like dreams. He does so in his paper on *Screen Memories*, published in 1899, but probably written after *The Interpretation of Dreams*.

Screen Memories

Freud begins this paper by pointing out that although impressions from our earliest years form 'ineradicable traces in the depths of our minds',[48] we are not able to access these directly in our conscious memory. Furthermore, he states that it is usually only in our sixth or seventh year, or even later, that we can remember our lives as a connected series of events. He presents the concept of a 'screen memory', one that is seemingly emotionally insignificant but is actually a substitute for a more troubling memory with which it bears an associative connection. Such a memory thus is partly determined by the mechanism of displacement which Freud had encountered in his study of dreams.

Freud presents an example of a memory described by a thirty-eight-year-old man (generally regarded as autobiographical). The narrator sees a rectangular sloping piece of meadow, green and thickly grown. There are yellow flowers, dandelions. A cottage stands at one end of the meadow, in front of which two women are chattering, a children's nurse and a peasant-woman. Three children are playing in the grass. One of these is the narrator, aged two or three, while the others are his boy cousin, aged a year older, and his cousin's sister who is the same age as the narrator. The children are picking the yellow flowers and each is holding a bunch, but the girl has the best bunch. The two boys fall on her and snatch the flowers. She runs away in tears and the peasant-woman gives her a big piece of bread. The narrator and his cousin throw away the flowers, hurry to the cottage and ask for some bread too. The peasant-woman cuts the bread with a long knife and gives them some. The bread tastes delicious.

The account of the memory does have a dream-like quality and Freud employs exactly the same principles as he does for dream interpretation, exploring associations to the various details and eventually explaining the 'memory' in terms of repressed wishes and phantasies. His exploration of the memory is lengthy. However, its meaning emerges as the narrator recalls the vivid yellow dress of a girl he fell in love with at age seventeen, linking to the yellow of the flowers. The girl, whose family were wealthy, lived in the country. Originally the narrator lived in the same area near beautiful woods, but after his father's business collapsed they had to leave and live in relative poverty in the town. Three years after his encounter with the girl with the yellow dress at age seventeen, he visited his uncle and met the two other children who appeared in the memory. His father and uncle came up with a plan whereby he would give up his abstruse studies for a more practical career, marry his cousin (with the yellow flowers) and settle down in the area where his uncle lived. The narrator had not pursued this plan because he preferred to continue his chosen studies.

Freud's interpretation of the memory is as follows. The narrator had imagined the comfortable life he could have led if he had settled down along the lines of the plan proposed by his father and uncle, but if instead of marrying his cousin (as they suggested) he had married the girl in the yellow dress. This pleasant life was represented by the delicious bread. Taking flowers from the girl represented 'deflowering' her, an act that would have contrasted with his bashful attitude during his original encounter with her. Throwing away the flowers represented a wishful idea of throwing away his unpractical ideas and following the 'bread and butter' occupation presented by his father. This wishful phantasy memory emerged during a period when the narrator was working particularly hard and indeed struggling for his 'daily bread'.

In response to this interpretation, the narrator comments:

It seems that I amalgamated the two sets of phantasies of how my life could have been more comfortable – the 'yellow' and the 'country-made-bread' from the one and the throwing-away of the flowers and the actual people concerned from the other.

Freud replies:

Yes. You projected the two phantasies on to one another and made a childhood memory of them . . . I can assure you that people often construct such things unconsciously – almost like works of fiction.[49]

Thus, Freud has hypothesised that the memory is *constructed* as a wishful phantasy driven by current difficulties in the narrator's life, and that it combines and condenses elements from different sources, using metaphor and pun, just as do dreams. The implication is not only that apparent memories are deceptive and essentially dream-like, but that they may be *created* in response to current difficulties.

Freud concludes his paper by arguing that the distinction between screen memories and other memories from childhood may not be a clear one. He makes the following astonishing statement:

It may indeed be questioned whether we have any memories at all from our childhood: memories relating to our childhood may be all that we possess. Our childhood memories show us our earliest years not as they were but as they appeared at the later periods when the memories were aroused. In these periods of arousal, the childhood memories did not, as people are accustomed to say, emerge; they were formed at that time. And a number of motives, with no concern for historical accuracy, had a part in forming them, as well as in the selection of the memories themselves.[50]

Thus Freud argues that memories of childhood may be not what they seem – that the subjective sense of remembering does not mean that the memory is literally true. Memories are like dreams, he says, or like works of fiction, constructed out of psychodynamic conflict, serving wish-fulfilment and self-deception. They combine elements from different sources, without regard for truth or reality. True memories of childhood may simply be unobtainable, he suggests. Our apparent memories may be fabrications created later.

Freud on Reconstruction in Psychoanalysis

Some of Freud's comments on the process of reconstruction, whereby the analyst speculatively builds a picture of the patient's early development on the basis of clues provided in free-association and behaviour in the consulting room, may have acted as another possible source of the assumption that he believed that video-like representations of early events were preserved in memory, always potentially available for conscious recall if the right method is used. For example, in his paper *Constructions in Analysis* (1937), Freud presents his familiar archaeological metaphor, arguing that both analyst and archaeologist are attempting to reconstruct the image of the original structure on the basis of whatever clues are available. However, he claims that the psychoanalyst works under more favourable conditions because unlike the archaeologist who is dealing with objects that might be lost or damaged, the analyst's 'psychical object' is not destroyed:

All of the essentials are preserved; even things that seem completely forgotten are present somehow and somewhere, and have merely been buried and made inaccessible to the subject.[51]

It could, on first reading, be assumed that Freud meant the psychoanalyst's search was for a buried 'psychical object', such as a memory of an event, a trauma such as sexual abuse. However, what Freud actually gives as a hypothetical example of reconstruction of a forgotten piece of the patient's early history is as follows:

Up to your nth year you regarded yourself as the sole and unlimited possessor of your mother; then came another baby and brought you grave disillusionment. Your mother left you for some time, and even after her reappearance she was never again devoted to you exclusively. Your feelings towards your mother again became ambivalent, your father gained a new importance for you . . . [52]

Thus although Freud is here referring to a verifiable external event – the arrival of a baby – this external event is not in itself the focus of the reconstruction. It is not this 'fact' that was reconstructed. The 'psychical object' is a complex constellation of the patient's feelings, phantasies and illusions, especially that of being the sole possessor of his mother. This psychical object cannot be directly observed; it can never be verified by an external observer, but can only be evaluated by patient and analyst together as they attempt to understand how remnants of past mental life continue to invade the present. The existence of the psychical object is inferred from clues in the patient's current presentation in the consulting room. Freud is describing the reconstruction not of external but of internal events, essentially the data of introspection and empathy.

Freud's Concept of Repression

Although a crucial Freudian concept and one that has been made central at times in the debate about false memory, this topic is left until last because it is in many ways the most simple. Freud's 'cornerstone on which the whole structure of psycho-analysis rests'[53] is his observation that certain contents of the mind can be repudiated, or banished from consciousness, only to reappear, in disguised form, as dreams, symptoms, slips of the tongue, accidents or exaggerated character traits. This basic idea has enormous explanatory power, but does it imply some very obscure, mysterious or counter-intuitive process? Here is how Freud defined it in his 1915 paper, *Repression*:

The essence of repression lies simply in turning something away, and keeping it at a distance, from the conscious . . .[54]

Although, by definition, once repressed a mental content becomes unconscious, Freud's definition does not imply that the process of repression is necessarily completely unconscious to begin with, nor that it is completely successful. It could well start with a person's deliberate effort to put something painful out of their mind, or not to think about it. This is not unusual or mysterious. Cognitive therapists call this 'cognitive avoidance'.

This point is important because some commentators in the memory debate engage in a piece of circular reasoning, whereby it is said that there is no evidence for repression in a particular case because there is no reason to assume that a person's forgetting, or not knowing, was anything more than a preferring not to know or not to think about a certain thing.[55]

While it is true that Freud did postulate further subtle distinctions between 'primal repression' and 'repression proper', these need not overly concern us here. He proposed a combination of forces acting in repression: a repulsion from the consciousness above (repression proper) and an attraction, a pull downwards from the unconscious, exercised by the primally repressed. However, Freud did not provide any clinical material that could illustrate what led him to this distinction – and it is one that has never held any clinical meaning for this writer.

Repression of What?

What is repressed? Freud begins his paper as follows:

One of the vicissitudes an instinctual impulse may undergo is to meet with resistances which seek to make it inoperative . . . the impulse passes into the state of 'repression'.[56]

So, by 1915 Freud was clearly concerned primarily with repression not of memory but of instinctual impulses. It is precisely because there can be no external flight from an instinct, which continually presses for expression, that repression is necessary and must be maintained. However, once repressed and thereby withdrawn from conscious influence, the impulse develops with less interference.

It proliferates in the dark, as it were, and takes on extreme forms of expression . . .[57]

Derivatives of the repressed will leak back into consciousness if they are sufficiently removed from the primally repressed, finding expression in symptoms, dreams, free-associations and all the numerous forms of 'psychopathology of everyday life'. This, in essence, was Freud's theory.

Conclusion: Freud on Memory and Abuse

Freud discovered that psychodynamic conflict – opposition between emotional forces within the mind – can result in neurotic (hysterical) symptoms, which function both to conceal and express an unacceptable idea or impulse. He found that such conflicts often involved sexuality in one form or another. For a brief period of a year or so, he believed that hysteria rested ultimately upon repressed (forgotten) experiences of sexual abuse in childhood. His method of 'analysis' at that time involved quite coercive efforts to persuade patients to follow their chains of association. He believed that he had to expend analytic work against the patient's resistance. Today, such methods would be considered likely to contribute to confabulated images, falsely perceived as memories.

Freud was not unaware of this, since his early papers contained much discussion of such possibilities. However, he soon decided, after a painful inner struggle, that he had been mistaken; not all the apparent memories he thought he had recovered from repression could be true. He began to turn his attention to 'psychic reality', the inner world of instincts, wishes and phantasies. Shortly after giving up the 'seduction theory', Freud began writing his book on dreams, illustrating how the mind inherently contains the capacity for self-deception which is continually at work. He also wrote his paper on 'screen memories', arguing that memories of childhood may not be genuine memories at all, but instead later constructions, retrospectively attributed to the distant past. He showed that memories can be like dreams or works of fiction – and that the subjective experience of remembering is no guarantee of the literal truth of a memory.

Taking apart the illusions of conscious intention and knowledge still further, he wrote about the psychopathology of everyday life, the innumerable ways in which unconscious wishes and thoughts are expressed in disguised form through slips of the tongue, errors, accidents, forgetting and so forth. He showed how even the most firmly and fervently held beliefs, such as those of religion, may rest upon unconscious and repressed infantile foundations. As he once commented, referring to his own feelings of bewilderment at times during his work: 'The firm ground of reality was gone.'[58]

Freud did find evidence, for example in dreams, that knowledge and memory not available to the conscious mind appeared to be stored in some form unconsciously. However, he also – and this is absolutely crucial – emphasised the ways in which memories of experiences, especially those of long ago, are subject to all manner of distortion, mixing elements from different sources, and are rarely available to conscious recall in coherent and accurate form.

In this way, Freud's views of memory, as well as his understanding of the impact of childhood sexual abuse, seem remarkably in tune with today's perspectives. Moreover, in drawing attention to the quicksands beneath many of our apparent certainties and realities, Freud could more accurately be regarded as the father of postmodernism rather than of 'the recovered memory fad'.

It is well over a hundred years since a 19th-century Viennese neurologist first began writing about psychoanalysis – the study of the mind's capacity to deceive itself. Here at the dawn of the 21st century, still he seems to bother us.

Psychoanalysis since Freud

Freud died in London in 1939. Since then, psychoanalysis has continued to be a field of lively intellectual, clinical and scientific debate and exploration. Many areas of research have enriched the analyst's understanding – for example, studies of early attachment and its disturbances. Today in Britain there are several university departments of psychoanalytic studies. Psychoanalysts have gradually been able to describe and understand increasingly complex and subtle processes of emotion and phantasy, occurring both within the individual mind and between people. Although full psychoanalysis, as a five-times-per-week treatment for several years, remains time-consuming and expensive, there are many briefer applications of psychoanalysis (psychoanalytic psychotherapy) which are widely practised. In Britain, the Tavistock Clinic has for many years been a centre of excellence for clinical research based on psychoanalysis and for the application of psychoanalysis to the National Health Service. Research on psychoanalytic outcome is complex, but a survey of forty-seven studies from around the world, commissioned by the International Psychoanalytic Association, shows good results in many cases.[59]

Training in psychoanalysis is lengthy and is not normally undertaken until a person's late thirties. Candidates come from a variety of backgrounds, including medicine, clinical psychology, social work, anthropology or other professions involving studying and helping people. In Britain, psycho-analysts are trained by the Institute of Psycho-Analysis. Its associated London Clinic of Psycho-analysis offers low-cost psychoanalysis.[60]

In addition, there are a number of trainings in psychoanalytic psychotherapy. These can be found listed in the register of the British Confederation of Psychotherapists.

In the USA, institutes of psychoanalysis can be found in most major cities.

What Happens in Psychoanalysis Today?

Although there are many variations of style and nuances of theory among analysts around the world, the prospective patient can expect the fol-lowing. He or she will have the option of lying on a couch (although a chair will be available), while the analyst sits behind. The invitation will be to speak of whatever comes to mind, while the analyst listens thoughtfully with a freely-floating attentiveness. As the analyst gradually discerns patterns of emotional conflict embedded in the patient's free-associative discourse, these may be formulated for the patient as tentative *interpretations* or hypotheses. Of par-ticular significance may be the patient's emotional conflicts as these become manifest in relation to the analyst. The analytic stance is one of tolerating uncertainty, creating an ambience in which aspects of self and experience can be explored without an anxious rushing to conclusions. The famous British psychoanalyst, Wilfred Bion, likened this to Keats' idea of Negative Capability:

. . . that is, when a man is capable of being in un-certainties, mysteries, doubts, without any irritable reaching after fact and reason.[61]

A Caution Regarding False Memories

There are no known methods of reliably enhancing memory. Attempts to do so run the risk of yielding confabulated or false memories. Hypnosis and related methods should not be used to elicit 'repressed memories'. Without objective corroboration, it may be impossible to determine whether a recovered memory – that is, an experience that had been firmly forgotten and then later remembered – is essentially true or is a product of imagination.

Notes

1. E. Loftus, and K. Ketcham, *The Myth of Repressed Memory: False Memories and Allegations of Sexual Abuse*, New York: St. Martin's Press, 1994.

2. K. Pope, 'Memory, abuse and science: Questioning claims about the false memory syndrome epidemic', *American Psychologist*, September, 1996, pp. 957–74.

3. D. Brown, A.W. Scheflin and D.C. Hammond, *Memory, Trauma Treatment and the Law*, New York: Norton, 1998, pp. 1–2.

4. P. Mollon, *Remembering Trauma: A Psychotherapist's Guide to Memory and Illusion*, Chichester: Wiley, 1998.

5. R. Ofshe, and E. Watters, *Making Monsters: False Memories, Psychotherapy and Sexual Hysteria*, London: Andre Deutsch, 1995, p. 294.

6. F. Crews, *The Memory Wars: Freud's Legacy in Dispute*, London: Granta, 1997, p. 9.

7. J. Breuer and S. Freud, *Studies on Hysteria, Standard Edition of the Complete Psychological Works of Sigmund Freud* II , London: Hogarth Press, 1893–1895.

8. D. Schacter, *Searching for Memory*, New York: Basic Books, 1996, p. 274.

9. J. Breuer and S. Freud, *Studies on Hysteria*, p. 117.

10. S. Freud, *Further Remarks on the Neuropsychoses of Defence, Standard Edition of the Complete Psychological Works of Sigmund Freud* III, London: Hogarth Press, 1896a, p. 162.

11. Ibid., p. 163.

12. Ibid., p. 164.

13. Ibid., p. 166.

14. S. Freud, *Project for a Scientific Psychology, Standard Edition of the Complete Psychological Works of Sigmund Freud* I, London: Hogarth Press, 1895, p. 354.

15. S. Freud, *Further Remarks on the Neuropsychoses of Defence.*

16. Ibid., p. 172.

17. Ibid., p. 178.

18. Ibid., p. 183.

19. Ibid., p. 164.

20. S. Freud, *The Aetiology of Hysteria, Standard Edition of the Complete Psychological Works of Sigmund Freud* III, London: Hogarth Press, 1896b, p. 212.

21. Ibid., p. 193.

22. Ibid., p. 199.

23. Ibid., pp. 202–3.

24. Ibid., p. 214.

25. Ibid., p. 215.

26. Ibid., p. 220.

27. Ibid., p. 220.

28. Ibid., p. 205.

29. Ibid., p. 208.

30. Ibid., p. 208.

31. Ibid., p. 204.

32. Ibid., p. 204.

33. Ibid., p. 204.

34. Ibid., p. 208.

35. J. Breuer and S. Freud, *Studies on Hysteria, Standard Edition of the Complete Psychological Works of Sigmund Freud* II, London: Hogarth Press, 1893–1895, p. 281.

36. S. Freud, *The Aetiology of Hysteria*, p. 204.

37. S. Freud, *Further Remarks on the Neuropsychoses of Defence*, p. 168.

38. S. Freud, *On the History of the Psycho-Analytical Movement, Standard Edition of the Complete Psychological Works of Sigmund Freud* XIV, London: Hogarth Press, 1914, p. 17.

39. Ibid., p. 17.

40. F. Crews, *The Memory Wars: Freud's Legacy in Dispute*, London: Granta, 1997; A. Esterson, *Seductive Mirage: An Exploration of the Work of Sigmund Freud*, New York: Open Court, 1993.

41. S. Freud, *Moses and Monotheism, Standard Edition of the Complete Psychological Works of Sigmund Freud* XXIII, London, Hogarth Press, 1939, pp. 75–6.

42. S. Freud, *An Outline of Psycho-Analysis, Standard Edition of the Complete Psychological Works of Sigmund Freud* XXIII, London: Hogarth Press, 1940, p. 276.

43. S. Freud, *Introductory Lectures on Psycho-Analysis, Standard Edition of the Complete Psychological Works of Sigmund Freud* XVI, London: Hogarth Press, 1917, p. 367.

44. S. Freud, *An Outline of Psycho-Analysis*, p. 187.

45. Ibid., p. 187.

46. S. Freud, *The Interpretation of Dreams, Standard Edition of the Complete Psychological Works of Sigmund Freud* IV, London: Hogarth Press, 1900, p. 14.

47. S. Freud, *On the History of the Psycho-Analytical Movement*, p. 20.

48. S. Freud, *Screen Memories, Standard Edition of the Complete Psychological Works of Sigmund Freud* III, London: Hogarth Press, 1899, p. 303.

49. Ibid., p. 315.

50. Ibid., p. 322.

51. S. Freud, *Constructions in Analysis, Standard Edition of the Complete Psychological Works of Sigmund Freud* XXIII, London: Hogarth Press, 1937, p. 260.

52. Ibid., p. 261.

53. S. Freud, *On the History of the Psycho-Analytical Movement*, p. 16.

54. S. Freud, *Repression, Standard Edition of the Complete Psychological Works of Sigmund Freud* XIV, London: Hogarth Press, 1915, p. 147.

55. H. Pope and J. Hudson, 'Can memories of childhood sexual abuse be repressed?', *Psychological Medicine* (25), 1995, pp. 121–6.

56. S. Freud, *Repression*, p. 146.

57. Ibid., p. 149.

58. S. Freud, *On the History of the Psycho-Analytical Movement*, p. 17.

59. International Psychoanalytic Association, *An Open Door Review of Outcomes Studies in Psychoanalysis*,

London: IPA, 1999.

60. Further information can be gained by visiting website: http://www.psychoanalysis.org.uk

61. W.R. Bion, *Attention and Interpretation*, London: Tavistock 1970, p. 125; reprinted by Karnac, London, 1984.

Bibliography

Bion, W. R., *Attention and Interpretation*, London: Tavistock 1970; reprinted by Karnac, London, 1984.

Breuer, J. and Freud, S., *Studies on Hysteria, Standard Edition of the Complete Psychological Works of Sigmund Freud* II, London: Hogarth Press, 1893–1895.

Brown, D., Scheflin, A. W. and Hammond, D. C., *Memory, Trauma Treatment and the Law*, New York: Norton, 1998.

Crews, F., *The Memory Wars: Freud's Legacy in Dispute*, London: Granta, 1997.

Esterson, A., *Seductive Mirage: An Exploration of the Work of Sigmund Freud*, New York: Open Court, 1993.

Freud, S., *Project for a Scientific Psychology, Standard Edition of the Complete Psychological Works of Sigmund Freud* I, London: Hogarth Press, 1895.

Freud, S., *Further Remarks on the Neuropsychoses of Defence, Standard Edition of the Complete Psychological Works of Sigmund Freud* III, London: Hogarth Press, 1896a.

Freud, S., *The Aetiology of Hysteria, Standard Edition of the Complete Psychological Works of Sigmund Freud* III, London: Hogarth Press, 1896b.

Freud, S., *Screen Memories, Standard Edition of the Complete Psychological Works of Sigmund Freud* III,

London: Hogarth Press, 1899.

Freud, S., *The Interpretation of Dreams, Standard Edition of the Complete Psychological Works of Sigmund Freud* IV, London: Hogarth Press, 1900.

Freud, S., *On the History of the Psycho-Analytical Movement, Standard Edition of the Complete Psychological Works of Sigmund Freud* XIV, London: Hogarth Press, 1914.

Freud, S., *Repression, Standard Edition of the Complete Psychological Works of Sigmund Freud* XIV, London: Hogarth Press, 1915.

Freud, S., *Introductory Lectures on Psycho-Analysis, Standard Edition of the Complete Psychological Works of Sigmund Freud* XVI, London: Hogarth Press, 1917.

Freud, S., *Constructions in Analysis, Standard Edition of the Complete Psychological Works of Sigmund Freud* XXIII, London: Hogarth Press, 1917.

Freud, S., *Moses and Monotheism, Standard Edition of the Complete Psychological Works of Sigmund Freud* XXIII, London, Hogarth Press, 1939.

Freud, S., *An Outline of Psycho-Analysis, Standard Edition of the Complete Psychological Works of Sigmund Freud* XXIII, London: Hogarth Press, 1940.

Freyd, J. J., *Betrayal Trauma: The Logic of Forgetting Childhood Abuse*, Cambridge MA: Harvard University Press, 1996.

International Psychoanalytic Association, *An Open Door*

Review of Outcomes Studies in Psychoanalysis, London: IPA, 1999.

Loftus, E. and Ketcham, K., *The Myth of Repressed Memory: False Memories and Allegations of Sexual Abuse*, New York: St. Martin's Press, 1994.

Masson, J., *Freud: The Assault on Truth*, London: Faber & Faber, 1984.

Mollon, P., *Remembering Trauma: A Psychotherapist's Guide to Memory and Illusion*, Chichester: Wiley, 1998.

Ofshe, R. and Watters, E., *Making Monsters: False Memories, Psychotherapy and Sexual Hysteria*, London: Andre Deutsch, 1995.

Pope, K., 'Memory, abuse and science: Questioning claims about the false memory syndrome epidemic', *American Psychologist*, September, 1996, pp. 957–74.

Pope, H. and Hudson, J., 'Can memories of childhood sexual abuse be repressed?' *Psychological Medicine* (25), 1995.

Sandler, J. and Fonagy, P. (eds.), *Recovered Memories of Abuse: True or False?*, London: Karnac, 1996.

Schacter, D., *Searching for Memory*, New York: Basic Books, 1996.

Sinason, V. (ed.), *Memory in Dispute*, London: Karnac, 1998.

Wakefield, H. and Underwager, R., *Return of the Furies: An Investigation into Recovered Memory Therapy*, Chicago: Open Court, 1994.

Other titles available in the Postmodern Encounters series from Icon/Totem

Derrida and the End of History
Stuart Sim
ISBN 1 84046 094 6
UK £2.99   USA $7.95

What does it mean to proclaim 'the end of history', as several thinkers have done in recent years? Francis Fukuyama, the American political theorist, created a considerable stir in *The End of History and the Last Man* (1992) by claiming that the fall of communism and the triumph of free market liberalism brought an 'end of history' as we know it. Prominent among his critics has been the French philosopher Jacques Derrida, whose *Specters of Marx* (1993) deconstructed the concept of 'the end of history' as an ideological confidence trick, in an effort to salvage the unfinished and ongoing project of democracy.

Derrida and the End of History places Derrida's claim within the context of a wider tradition of 'endist' thought. Derrida's critique of endism is highlighted as one of his most valuable contributions to the postmodern cultural debate – as well as being the most accessible entry to *deconstruction*, the controversial philosophical movement founded by him.

Stuart Sim is Professor of English Studies at the University of Sunderland. The author of several works on critical and cultural theory, he edited *The Icon Critical Dictionary of Postmodern Thought* (1998).

Foucault and Queer Theory
Tamsin Spargo

ISBN 1 84046 092 X
UK £2.99   USA $7.95

Michel Foucault is the most gossiped-about celebrity of French poststructuralist theory. The homophobic insult 'queer' is now proudly reclaimed by some who once called themselves lesbian or gay. What is the connection between the two?

This is a postmodern encounter between Foucault's theories of sexuality, power and discourse and the current key exponents of queer thinking who have adopted, revised and criticised Foucault. Our understanding of gender, identity, sexuality and cultural politics will be radically altered in this meeting of transgressive figures.

Foucault and Queer Theory excels as a brief introduction to Foucault's compelling ideas and the development of queer culture with its own outspoken views on heteronormativity, sado-masochism, performativity, transgender, the end of gender, liberation-versus-difference, late capitalism and the impact of AIDS on theories and practices.

Tamsin Spargo worked as an actor before taking up her current position as Senior Lecturer in Literary and Historical Studies at Liverpool John Moores University. She writes on religious writing, critical and cultural theory and desire.

Nietzsche and Postmodernism
Dave Robinson

ISBN 1 84046 093 8
UK £2.99   USA $7.95

Friedrich Nietzsche (1844–1900) has exerted a huge influence on 20th century philosophy and literature – an influence that looks set to continue into the 21st century. Nietzsche questioned what it means for us to live in our modern world. He was an 'anti-philosopher' who expressed grave reservations about the reliability and extent of human knowledge. His radical scepticism disturbs our deepest-held beliefs and values. For these reasons, Nietzsche casts a 'long shadow' on the complex cultural and philosophical phenomenon we now call 'postmodernism'.

Nietzsche and Postmodernism explains the key ideas of this 'Anti-Christ' philosopher. It then provides a clear account of the central themes of postmodernist thought exemplified by such thinkers as Derrida, Foucault, Lyotard and Rorty, and concludes by asking if Nietzsche can justifiably be called the first great postmodernist.

Dave Robinson has taught philosophy for many years. He is the author of Icon/Totem's introductory guides to Philosophy, Ethics and Descartes. He thinks that Nietzsche is a postmodernist, but he's not sure.

Baudrillard and the Millennium
Christopher Horrocks
ISBN 1 84046 091 1
UK £2.99   USA $7.95

'In a sense, we do not believe in the Year 2000', says French thinker Jean Baudrillard. Still more disturbing is his claim that the millennium might not take place. Baudrillard's analysis of 'Y2K' reveals a repentant culture intent on storing, mourning and laundering its past, and a world from which even the possibility of the 'end of history' has vanished. Yet behind this bleak vision of integrated reality, Baudrillard identifies enigmatic possibilities and perhaps a final ironic twist.

Baudrillard and the Millennium confronts the strategies of this major cultural analyst's encounter with the greatest non-event of the postmodern age, and accounts for the critical censure of Baudrillard's enterprise. Key topics, such as natural catastrophes, the body, 'victim culture', identity and Internet viruses, are discussed in reference to the development of Jean Baudrillard's millenarian thought from the 1980s to the threshold of the Year 2000 – from simulation to disappearance.

Christopher Horrocks is Senior Lecturer in Art History at Kingston University in Surrey. His publications include *Introducing Baudrillard* and *Introducing Foucault*, both published by Icon/Totem. He lives in Tulse Hill, in the south of London.